We Build A HOUSE

MICHELLE BEACHY
(through the eyes of Adam)

We Build a House ISBN: 978-1-932676-21-1

Cover and Text Design: Lonnie D. Yoder

For additional copies or comments write to:

Vision Publishers • P.O. Box 190 • Harrisonburg, VA 22803

Fax: 540/437-1969 • Phone: 877/488-0901

E-mail: orders@vision-publishers.com

www.vision-publishers.com

Hello Parents,

Welcome to an exciting new series of books from Vision Publishers aimed at helping children adjust to changes in life!

As children grow, they are bound to discover that life inevitably brings changes. These changes can be unsettling experiences to young children, but they can also be stepping stones as they look back and see parental love and God's faithfulness through all of life.

In this first book, *We Build a House*, journey with little Adam through the experience of the family building a new house. Children will enjoy the many color pictures throughout the book, as they look at the move through the eyes of a little one. They will also see that Adam can adjust to this change because of the love and security he feels in his home.

Daddy, Mommy, and I are building a house for our family. We have a house now, but Mommy says someone else owns it. The house we live in now is very small. It is just right for the three of us.

When we go out to our property, I just see a lot of trees and dirt. I wonder how we will make a house? One day, a man came with a front loader. Daddy cut down trees and the man pushed them together with his big machine. Then he started to dig a big hole in the ground. He made huge piles of dirt. Mommy says that in the hole is where we will build the basement. I love to watch the front loader. It made me cry when Mommy said it was time to go home for my nap.

Our basement walls came in pieces on a flat-bed truck. The men used a crane to position them and then bolted them together.

Mommy took me to the new house again another day so that we could watch the concrete truck. They put the concrete in wheelbarrows and dumped it out to spread over the gravel. When they were cleaning up the truck, the man sprayed me with water, too! That was fun!

I love to go to the new house. There are so many things to watch.

It's fun to play at the new house, but it still doesn't look very much like a house to me. Mommy and Daddy are talking about "framing." Daddy went out to the new house by himself tonight. Mommy and I are making cinnamon rolls for the people who are coming to help us.

When Mommy and I went to the house the next day, the noise was loud. Mommy had to use her very big voice so I could hear her above the generator. I heard a chop saw and lots of power nailers and an air compressor. I liked those noises. Someday I want to help build a house.

When lunch was ready, the men stopped working and turned all the noisy machines off. They were all hot and sweaty and ready for a break. I was hot too. I have a little chair like Daddy has a big chair and I got to sit with him to eat lunch. I like to see daddy working on the house.

After lunch, Darius gave us a ride on the lift. Up, up, up all the way to the top of the house. It felt like we were going up to the sky. I didn't even feel scared.

I like to walk around with my cousins, Marilyn and Rochelle, to watch our daddies and the other men work. Mommy says we need to be careful to stay far away. The saws are dangerous, and the men drive the lift very fast. Sometimes they throw boards down off the roof, and we could get hurt.

To build the roof, the men used trusses that looked like this.

Grandpa hooked them to the end of a rope. Then, a big crane picked them up and swung them onto the top of the house.

It looks more like the shape of a house now.

Now our house has an inside and an outside. It has doors, windows, and even bathtubs.

Daddy and Mommy let me help them use tools to do big jobs. Sometimes we meet Daddy at the new house after he gets off work. We work 'til bedtime. Every Saturday I get to work with my daddy at our new house.

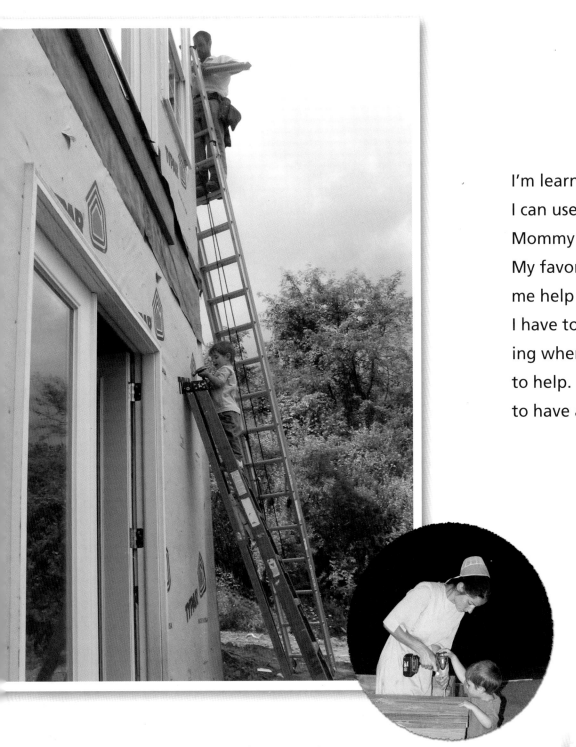

I'm learning so many new things! I can use sandpaper and hammers. Mommy lets me help use the drill. My favorite part is when Daddy lets me help him cut a board. Sometimes I have to be happy with just watching when it's too dangerous for me to help. Mommy says it's important to have a good attitude anyway.

It seems as though we've been building our house for such a long time, and yet we're not finished. I still like to go work there. Sometimes Daddy and Mommy say I need to stay with a babysitter because they are doing jobs that are too dangerous for me. I like going to Grandma's house; but I like going to work with Daddy even better.

Things are different now when we are at home. Daddy and Mommy are often busy. Sometimes when we get home they say, "It's too late to play truck tonight." I like Sunday afternoons because we go on walks down to the bridge and throw sticks into the water.

Big things are happening at our house again. A lot of men from our church came to help Daddy put siding on the house. Now the outside is white instead of gray with writing on it. In three days they had almost all the siding done. Daddy keeps saying "thank you so much" to the men who come to help. It's kind of them to help us the same as it's kind when I share my toys. Mommy says God's love makes us want to share. I guess these men feel happy in their hearts the same as I do.

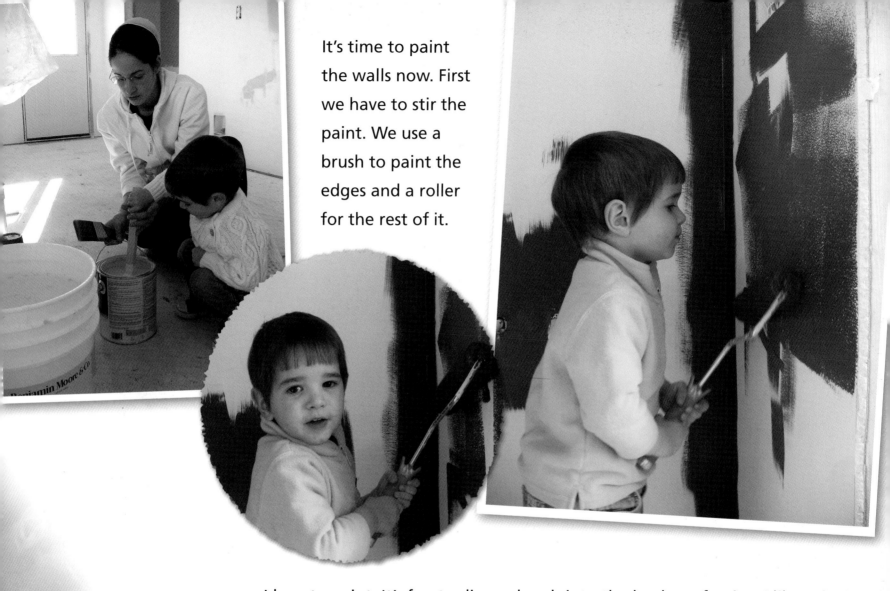

It's time to paint the walls now. First we have to stir the paint. We use a brush to paint the edges and a roller for the rest of it.

I love to paint. It's fun to dip my brush into the bucket of paint. I like using a roller, too. Mommy says we have to paint evenly. We shouldn't have any thick runners and no skipped areas. I like to watch the wall change color. My room is going to be yellow, almost like the kitchen. I like yellow. Actually, I like all the colors in our house.

My daddy is a very good carpenter. Sometimes when I'm at home, I pretend I'm a carpenter, too. I use an ice chest for my table saw and a yardstick for a board. I like to build things.

We are almost finished enough with the inside of our new house to move! Daddy put the trim up around the windows and doors, and we have cabinets in our kitchen and bathrooms. There are still things I may help with, but I have to be careful to only use tools where Daddy says I may. Tools help us to build things, but they can also ruin things if we use them on wood that is finished. I like to help sand. I can blow the dust off just like Daddy does.

Things are starting to look different at our old house. Mommy and I are pulling everything out of all the closets and the attic to get ready to move to our new house. Sometimes we find treasures! Mommy let me try on her graduation cap and gown when we found it in the attic.

Mommy says that moving means we will take all of our things from the old house to the new house. We'll take my bed, and my toys, and all my trucks, Mommy's dishes, and our couch and chairs and table and everything. Even my dog, Goldie. Then we won't live here anymore. That means we will always be at the new house, even to sleep.

Moving day is here! Lots of men came and loaded our furniture onto their trucks. I didn't know beds come apart, but they do. It makes it easier to take them places. When the men got to our new house, they put the pieces back together again. I liked watching the trucks come and seeing the men carry heavy chairs into our house.

Our new house looks like a house now. Mommy says we will sleep here tonight. I have the same bed I did at the other house. And Mommy made sure the sheep and fish I like to sleep with came here, too.

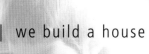

Sometimes I miss things from our old house like eating a picnic beside the pond or taking walks down to the creek.

I like living at our new house though. I have lots of room to ride my truck, and the park is only five minutes from our house. Our new neighbor has horses and we like to go pet them. Most important, Daddy and Mommy and I are all here, and that's what really matters. Sometime, I would like to build a house again. Mommy says when I'm a big man I can help Daddy build houses for other people. I would like that a lot.

Order More Books!

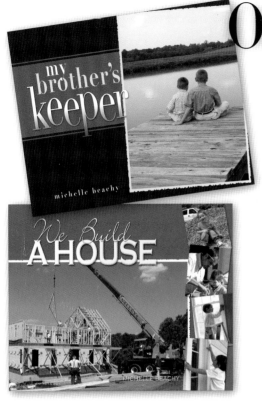

The Second Book in the Series

My Brother's Keeper

Hardcover - 24 pages - Full Color - 10 x 8 - $8.99 - ISBN: 978-1-932676-20-4

Join young Andrew Martin as he learns to adapt to life with a handicapped brother named Benjamin. Andrew discovers, as many children have, that not all changes in life are easy, but there are important lessons to be learned and to be thankful for.

I just wish Jesus still lived in Galilee. Then we could take Benjamin to see Jesus and he'd be well.

I used to pray and ask God to heal Benjamin. Then Mama told me this is God's plan for our lives. We don't know why, but God chose our family to take care of a special needs child. Now I pray that God would keep Benjamin from having a seizure while he sleeps and that He would help us take good care of Benjamin.

— *from the book*

Name _____ Phone _____ Date _____

Address_____ City_____ State_____ Zip_____

Send Completed Form to:

Vision Publishers

PO Box 190 · Harrisonburg, VA 22803 · 877.488.0901

fax: 540.437.1969 email: orders@vision-publishers.com

www.vision-publishers.com

☐Visa ☐Master Card ☐Discover ☐Money Order ☐ Check

3 digit code from signature panel ___ ___ ___ Name on card _____

Acct # _ _ _ _   _ _ _ _   _ _ _ _   _ _ _ _   Exp. Date _ _ _ _

Item #	Description	Qty. X Price	Amount
BRO76204	My Brother's Keeper	___ x $8.99	
HOU76211	We Build a House	___ x $8.99	
CHI00008	Set of 2 Books	___ x $16.99	
		Subtotal	
	VA Residents add 5% Sales Tax; OH Residents add Sales Tax for Your County	VA & OH Sales Tax	
	For S & H Please add a $3.00 Handling Charge Plus 10% of Subtotal	Shipping	
		Grand Total	

Price listed are in US dollars

Thank you for your order!